Comfort
and Joy

Simple Ways to Care for
Ourselves and Others

COLETTE LAFIA

ISBN: 9781573243513

Interior design by Brad Reynolds www.integralartandstudies.com

Cover illustration by Tyler Nilson

For my husband Mark, in gratitude for all
the comfort and love we continually share.

Comfort and Joy

Table of Contents

Comfort and Joy

Acknowledgments

I am deeply grateful to my family, friends, spiritual companions, and teachers who encouraged and supported me on the journey of writing this book. Your comfort, love, and support are at the heart of this project. Thank you.

I would like to thank Leslie Kirk Campbell, who worked with me on shaping the raw material of this book. A heartfelt thank you goes to Angeles Arrien for believing in my dreams and helping me to realize them. I would also like to thank Joanna Cotler for her insight and creative attention to this project.

I would like to thank Caroline Pincus and Jan Johnson, and the staff at Conari Press for all their great work on the first edition of this book. And a big thanks to Julie Isaac at WritingSpirit.com for being such a great coach and editor, and for her constant encouragement. A special thank you goes to my husband Mark, for all the moments of comfort and joy we have shared and continue to share together.

Comfort and Joy

Preface to the Revised Edition

*I*t is with great delight that I offer the revised and expanded edition of *Comfort and Joy: Simple Ways to Care for Ourselves and Others*. In this new edition, I've added journaling prompts, comfort meditations, and prayers to deepen your experience of, and connection to, the generous gifts that comfort has to offer. Over the years, I have come to appreciate how comfort is a way of applying spirituality and nurturing to our everyday lives.

When this book came out in 2008, my father had just passed away. I was so grateful that he'd had a chance to read the book, and found comfort in it. He called one day and left me a message, "I really get what you're saying, and it's so important."

Now, eight years later, I've recently lost my mother, and I'm feeling a deep need for comfort, once again. In fact, I notice how natural these comfort practices feel during difficult times, when our body and heart calls out for tenderness, mercy, and loving compassion towards ourselves and others.

Comfort and Joy has not only been a nurturing resource in my life, but has been a caring and calming influence in the lives of many others, as well. I remember one woman telling me that she saw the book on her daughter's bedside table for months, and that it helped soothe the stress that often arose from the busyness of her daughter's daily life. Another friend told me how her elderly aunt, who was in assisted living, kept the book on her bedside table for over a year. And I knew a woman whose sister carried the book in her purse as she dealt with her son's health issues, finding comfort to be a touchstone that kept her grounded in the midst of much uncertainty.

Comfort and Joy received the distinguished honor of being named one of The Best Spiritual Books of 2008 by Spirituality & Practice, alongside books by Deepak Chopra, Debbie Ford, Thomas Moore, Gary Chapman, Joyce Rupp, Matthew Fox, Jack Kornfield, and Br. David Steindl-Rast, among others. In their review, Frederic and Mary Ann Brussat wrote:

> *Comfort and Joy* contains a treasure trove of simple and pleasurable delights that lend meaning to our daily lives. Giving comfort to ourselves and bringing comfort to others is what we call the spiritual practice of nurturing.

Please enjoy the newly added comfort journal prompts, which you will find at the end of each vignette, as well as the new comfort meditations and prayers. You may want to commit to keeping a comfort journal in order to encourage and deepen your spiritual practice of nurturing both yourself and others.

How to Keep a Comfort Journal

Fill the paper with the breathings of your heart.

—William Wordsworth

What you will need:

1. *Select a journaling format that you like.* The size, shape, paper, and binding are all personal choices. Find something that feels inviting and comfortable. Whether you use a journal, notebook, or sketchpad, find something that feels inviting and comfortable.

2. *Select a variety of drawing and writing tools.* Include a variety of different colored pens, pencils, markers, oil pastels, or even a pack of crayons. I suggest that you take them out of their packages and boxes and keep them loose on a tray.

3. *Find a place to keep your journal.* Integrate your journal into your daily life. Leave it where it's easy to access—on a table, bookshelf, or desk.

4. *Create a writing ritual.* This can support your commitment to keeping a comfort journal. Try doing the writing at the same time every day (I like to do it first thing in the morning along with sipping a warm cup of tea). You can use something to help focus you like lighting a candle, saying a prayer, or through concentrating on your breath or simply being quiet for a few moments.

5. *Use the prompts I've provided, but feel free to change them and make them your own.* I recommend that you draw as well as write. It can bring more awareness, and it's fun. What I mean by drawing is simply making marks on the page—whatever lines, shapes, and colors have meaning for you, or an image that is symbolic.

The Daily Process:

- Before you begin, take three relaxing breaths—inhale and exhale—letting yourself feel each one as a way to settle into yourself.

- Be fully present in the moment with your journal. Have your writing and drawing tools available.

- Write at whatever time of day works best for you.

- Let inspiration be your guide and respond to the prompts that help you reflect upon your experiences in an authentic way.

- I encourage you to both write and draw in your journal as a way to discover what is deep within.

- After you're done, spend a few moments in gratitude for taking the time to write and draw in your journal, and for the feelings and thoughts that you received.

- Once a week, look over your journal as a way to integrate your experience. Notice what themes are emerging, and how your awareness of daily comfort and joy is increasing.

Comfort and Joy

Introduction: My Comfort Journey

*C*innamon toast, holding hands, the warmth of sand on bare feet, comfortable shoes, reading in bed, praying, drinking tea every morning, listening to a favorite song. These are some of the simple ways I found comfort during a difficult time in my life.

When I entered my thirties, I thought my life was on track. I was building a career in education, happily married and intending to have children, and writing fiction with the hope of finding a publisher. From the outside, my life looked rather routine and orderly.

But the order during those years was only on the surface. By my mid-thirties, my life began to exhibit chips and cracks, the way a clay bowl or cup does over time from use. I felt detached from my job, unfulfilled with my creative projects, and drained from years of struggling to conceive. During this time, my sister, who was only three years older than I, had been diagnosed with breast cancer. In addition to the struggles with my own life, I was faced with the confusion and grief I felt from the daily and intimate involvement with my sister's struggle and pain.

By the time I turned thirty-six, my sister had died, and the fragile bowl that held my spirit fell off the shelf and broke into tiny pieces. About six months later, I was sitting in my manager's office discussing my schedule for the new year when something in me snapped. "I can't do this anymore; I need to resign," I blurted out. She was startled, but not surprised, since my disengagement from my job had become apparent. I was relieved to be leaving a job I had outgrown, but the departure was also symbolic for me. I was walking out the door of a place I had entered with so many aspirations, and I was leaving empty-handed—no sister to talk to, no child to cradle, no book to hold.

My feelings of loss only increased in the following months, and I began to struggle with insomnia. In the sleepless nights that followed, I found myself in an unrecognizable landscape. Having trouble sleeping was completely foreign to me. I had always slept easily, anywhere and anytime—in a car, on a sofa, in a hotel. Sleep was something I could trust to give me relief and restore my energy, but now that had changed.

Sometimes, my husband would get up during the night and

try to soothe me. He would hold me, and in his arms I usually started crying. Often, we would share a mug of warm milk with honey while snuggled on the couch. In those moments, I recognized the first signs of comfort as I felt a relief, an ease, that made the fatigue less painful.

There was a calling in my body for comfort. I longed for it, cried for it, desired it. I needed to heal from all the pain accumulated in me, from my sister's cancer and dying process, the demands and disappointments of infertility treatments, and my deep feelings of being creatively unfulfilled.

I could not hide from what I was going through. As I shared my struggles with other people, they began to share their stories with me. Other people had lost loved ones to cancer. Other people had unfulfilled dreams. Other people had trouble sleeping. I felt comfort in these moments of exchange, of being listened to and of listening. By sharing everyday sufferings with other people, I was touching a depth in the human experience. In this way, I realized that I was not alone.

Comforting others was also a way of comforting myself. As I gave comfort, I received comfort. It was a turning wheel. Comfort could be felt in very simple ways— through a moment of listening, by a warm smile, from a gentle touch, or in a word of encouragement. To receive and give comfort was to trust both my capacity to give as well as my limits. I was craving to open this channel in myself and in others. Yet, could I accept it if someone didn't respond to my need, or have faith that I could always find comfort for myself? Could I become this vulnerable?

As I became more sensitive to my need for comfort, I began to recognize the many ways in which comfort was present in my daily life. I felt it in the softness of my clothes against my skin, in the scent of a fresh apple, and in the warmth of holding my husband's hand. Cultivating comfort in the ordinary moments of my daily life gave me tremendous relief, softness, nurturing, and support. The effects of comfort were like those of a pebble tossed into a pond. The rings multiplied, and the more I recognized the many ways that comfort restored me, the more comfort expanded into my daily life.

I was learning to be more receptive to my need for comfort. I didn't have to run away from it, or get over it, or find a way to change it. I just needed to listen, to pay attention, to hear what my body and heart were saying.

Still, the listening wasn't always easy, and was even harder in the night hours when I couldn't sleep, or as I continued not to conceive, or as I struggled with freelance work. How could I be patient and accepting of what I was going through?

In the darkness of the night, filled with uncertainty, and feeling vulnerable, I began scribbling in a large notebook. Within its pages, I began drawing a series of self-portraits in charcoal. I felt such comfort in these moments of expression. There was something in me that wanted to speak, something in me that was asking for my attention.

The night scribbling eventually led me to my first painting class. I had never painted before, but my instincts were pulling me in that direction. Surprisingly, I felt an intimacy when I painted, an intimacy that gave me comfort. From the beginning, painting gave me a deep way of listening to myself, and through this creative process, I began to rebuild a trust inside myself that had broken. Painting was part of a mending process, repairing the torn fibers of my soul's shawl.

There were stages in my comfort journey: feeling my need for comfort, recognizing the sources of comfort in my daily life, asking for comfort, and receiving it. Throughout the day and during the nights that I couldn't sleep, I would often ask myself, How can I find comfort right now?

With this attentiveness, I began to see how living comfort was a way to tap into my own internal healing process. I invited more comfort into my experiences, and over time I began to heal, to sleep better, and my husband and I resolved not to have children.

Comfort is a shelter, a warm blanket, a refuge. Fortunately, we do not need to do anything extraordinary to produce comfort, because it is something that already exists within each of us and all around us. Real comfort can be found in the context of daily living. It is a grace. We just need to open our arms and receive it. We just need to open our arms and give it.

I invite you to explore the power of comfort in your life. Your reasons for seeking comfort will be your own. I encourage you to bring them into the reading of these pages, and allow this book to open the doors of comfort in your daily life.

Comfort
Vignettes

Acceptance

I cannot think about life anymore. I just know that I'm asking another person to love me, in all my fragility. I just know that another person is asking me to love him, during a time of struggle. Sometimes, it's the will that gets tired, not the body. Comfort comes from feeling accepted. Comfort comes from accepting others.

For this one day, I will say: *This is enough, this is just right.* I will offer you my hand and encourage you on your journey. You will offer me your hand, and gently help me over the stepping stones of my path.

Together we lift each other up with the comfort of deep and willing acceptance.

Cultivating Comfort

Sometimes comfort isn't an action, but an open heart that you bring to a situation. Acceptance for others is rooted in accepting yourself. If you are tired today, emotionally vulnerable, or angry and frustrated, make room for it. Learn to gently say, I accept all of myself. I hold my feelings with tenderness, love, and comfort.

Journaling

Reflect upon and write about one area in your life in which you could be more accepting. What would that look and feel like?

Meditation & Prayer 💜

I place my hand over my heart, and breathe in acceptance for myself. I feel the presence of the Divine embracing me completely, just as I am.

A Bath

There are such things as comfort rituals—reading in bed, eating popcorn at the movies, listening to love songs.

The simple luxury of taking a bath is one of my favorite comfort rituals. I like preparing for a bath, setting the water to the right temperature, adding lavender bubble bath, lighting a few candles in the bathroom, and changing into my robe.

I like to linger before I get in the tub, letting my senses take in the sweet scent filling the bathroom, the amber glow of the candles, and the cool air on my skin. I step into the warm water, and sink my body into this royal experience. Comfort, felt deeply, sensuously, nurtures me in the core of my being.

Cultivating Comfort

Many sources of comfort are already available in your daily life. You need only to take time and recognize them. So the next time you take a bath, let it become a pool of comfort you are soaking in. Take a moment and reflect on what daily rituals comfort you. Notice them and appreciate the comfort they are giving you.

Journaling

Reflect upon and write about one of your favorite daily rituals and how it brings you comfort.

Meditation & Prayer

I contemplate with gratitude the daily rituals that continually give me comfort. May I savor these sacred moments and let them fill my heart with warmth and thankfulness.

A Bowl

A bowl, whether shallow or deep, small or large, wooden or ceramic, is always in the form of holding, receiving, and giving. A bowl is an opening. We display bowls in our houses for decoration. We place bowls at altars. We fill bowls.

A bowl full: of fruit, of a café au lait, or of clear water with a single gardenia floating in it.

What comfort there is in a bowl of soup on a chilly day.

What comfort there is in a bowl always offering something, like the wooden bowl on my coffee table, filled with roasted almonds, red grapes, or chocolates.

And what comfort there is in the beauty of a simple black bowl, made by a potter, sitting on the table, inviting us to fill it or leave it empty.

A bowl empty: of all that is not in it, of all that will come.

Cultivating Comfort

Comfort is both given and received, and like a bowl, you can be a vessel for that exchange. Are there bowls in your life that need to be emptied, in order to make more room for comfort to be received? Are there bowls in your life that need to be filled, so that you have more comfort to give?

Journaling

Reflect upon and write about the ways you open yourself to receiving comfort.

Meditation & Prayer

I hold in prayer the awareness that I am part of an infinite exchange of giving and receiving. May I be generous and give freely.

Calling

I walk into the Catholic church by my house. I have been walking into churches since I was a child, and the familiarity brings me comfort. The smells of incense and candles burning fill the air. There are always people praying, holding rosary beads, kneeling before statues, and lighting candles.

I feel the tremendous outpouring of prayers that have been said in this church. I have prayed here until I was speechless, and then my silence has prayed for me. There is comfort in not feeling alone and in joining in this communion.

We are calling, calling out to feel our glory, to reach beyond the tattered prayers on our tongues and dwell in the unbroken circle. We are the devotion of the body, reaching toward its divinity.

Cultivating Comfort

What place comforts you—a church, the woods, your grandmother's house? Take a moment and feel the calling you have to this place. If you cannot physically go there, then remember it—the colors, the smells, the feeling you have when you are there. If you can physically go to this place, then spend time there; don't rush, but rather linger, take in the smells, the sights, the feeling of comfort this place gives you.

Journaling

Reflect upon and write about the places where you find comfort.

Meditation & Prayer

I remember the special places in my life that comfort me—my home, my garden, and my favorite church. I hold these places close to my heart, knowing they're sacred places where I experience the divine.

Circles

There was a period of time in which I kept painting circles. Large black circles, small red circles, yellow circles intersecting with blue circles. I didn't have any particular meaning attached to them. It was simply comforting to paint circles. I liked the way my shoulder, arm, and wrist rolled when I painted a circle. I liked the feeling of going around and around on a piece of paper.

Soon my entire studio was filled with paintings of circles. Each circle felt like the whole world on a piece of paper: a world that was not fragmented, the way I experienced it every day. There was a perfection to the circle. Not perfect, but a perfection, as though life met not at its edges but in its center where it was round.

Cultivating Comfort

Circles are comforting. Did you ever notice that a hug is a circle? Circles remind us to look beyond beginnings and endings. They hold us in their roundness. Look around you and see how many things are formed in circles. Let comfort be a circle surrounding you.

Journaling

Reflect upon and write about a transition you are experiencing, and the ways that comfort is a circle holding you during this time.

Meditation & Prayer ♥

I pray to recognize that the arms of divine love are wrapped around me in a comforting circle. During times of transition and uncertainty, I trust that I am held in tenderness.

Clothes

We all have comfort clothes. They are flannel shirts, stretched-out sweaters, loose pants, soft pajamas, and cotton T-shirts. They are clothes that feel like another layer of skin, and when we put them on we instantly feel comfortable.

As soon as my husband and I get home from work, we immediately change into our comfort clothes. On a Saturday, we might wear them all day long, even out to the video store or the corner market. We'll wear these clothes over and over, until the elbows are thin, the buttons are loose, and the colors fade.

For years, I wore a green pair of corduroy pants, until finally it was time to let them go. I remember folding the pants with such reverence as I packed them into a cardboard box. There was a long history written in the creases of these pants. They had known me as I sat by my sister in the hospital, as I walked through the park in the wintertime, and as I ran my daily errands. These pants had given me comfort during so many moments of pain, enjoyment, and ordinary living.

We all have comfort clothes. We need to feel the body being touched with what knows us. Certain clothes bring us a deep comfort that is felt in our bones.

Cultivating Comfort

Clothes are an everyday source of comfort in your life. What touches your skin is very intimate and affects how you feel. Wearing a soft sweater can feel like having a cozy blanket wrapped around you all day. What clothes give you pure comfort?

Journaling

Reflect upon and write about the ways you are held in comfort by what you wear, both during the day and at night.

Meditation & Prayer ♥

May I notice all the comfort that my favorite clothes are giving me today, and allow the softness and familiarity to hold me and give me deep and nourishing comfort.

Creating

It is early morning, still dark outside. After tossing and turning for hours, I get out of bed and head to my art studio, which is tucked in the corner of the garage. I begin drawing, and as I press the charcoal into the white surface of the paper, I feel the warmth of comfort spread through my body. The intimacy of working with my hands softens my hardened bones, melting away the thick layer of tension that had built up during the restless night.

The morning light begins to appear, gracefully and deliberately like a dancer. And in that mood of awakening, I am drawing without hesitation. Pure instinct. Trusting every mark—a smudge, a smear, thick dark lines, thin gray lines. The drawing is already in me as I open my hands to receive it.

I draw as a way of listening, listening to something I cannot hear otherwise. I sometimes close my eyes when I draw and sink into not knowing. I feel the sensation of the charcoal pressing on the paper, sometimes with a feather-light touch, and other times with a forceful drag. It's in the listening that comfort can be heard. It is in a private moment of surrender that comfort can be received.

Cultivating Comfort

How can your creativity comfort you? Can gardening, painting, singing, writing, or cooking become a source of deep and nurturing comfort? Recognize and stay connected to the sources of creativity in your life.

Journaling

Reflect upon and write about how doing something creative brings you comfort, such as cooking, gardening, singing, writing, or drawing.

Meditation & Prayer

I pray to recognize the sacred in all the forms of creative expression I encounter today—in a painting, in a poem, in a psalm, or in the beauty of a piece of music.

The Garden

Sometimes, on a Saturday morning, there is nothing more satisfying than working in the garden. With hats and gloves on, my husband and I will work for hours in the backyard, as our appetites grow along with the rising sun. We will clip and prune the roses, shape the honeysuckle vines, and trim the sage bushes.

Our garden is a place where we can put our city hands into the earth and compost the feelings and thoughts of the week. We pull out weeds, like the little irritations that have stuck to us. We give everything a good watering, as we wash away our worries. We enjoy the blooms of the flowering plants, as we daydream about a poem or painting that is emerging on our desks.

We watch a butterfly, spot a spider's web, and add fresh soil to the clay pots. We fill the pots with new plants and anticipate their growth. We restore ourselves with the hope and beauty our garden contains.

When we are done, we sit on the wooden bench underneath the magnolia tree, appreciating the newly groomed garden and its gifts of beauty and comfort. Now, we are ready for a hearty weekend brunch.

Cultivating Comfort

A rosebush can teach you so much about life. Flowers bloom, and then wither away, until the next cycle of growth. Is there something in your life that needs you to see it as a cycle? Can you take comfort in this?

Journaling

Reflect upon and write about the ways you experience comfort in nature or in applying an awareness of the cycle of life to a personal situation.

Meditation & Prayer 🩶

I pray to notice the spirit of creation in all I see—in the vastness of the sky, in the variety of trees and leaves, and in a simple flower bud as it begins to bloom. I take time today to be grateful for the generosity of nature that surrounds me.

Giving

I reach into my bag and give the person on the sidewalk some food I am carrying. I reach for my cell phone to call my sister who's worried and looking for a new job. I pack a lunch to give my husband for his day. At times, we can give very basic expressions of comfort to others and to ourselves.

When I am having trouble sleeping, I give myself simple comforts. I might relax my feet with a warm wrap, hold my wooden rosary beads, or listen to a soothing piece of music. Most of all, I give myself the comforting gift of my patience.

There are always gifts of comfort to give and receive.

Cultivating Comfort

Moment by moment, and day to day, notice all the little ways you can give comfort to yourself and others.

Journaling

Reflect upon and write about the ways you can give yourself comfort today.

Meditation & Prayer

I pray to recognize the simple ways I can give comfort to those around me, and to remember that I can do small things with great love.

The Guitar

My husband cradles the guitar in his arms. He strums. He picks. The repetition of a chord rocks him and brings him ease. The music stops his worrying and soothes his body. He feels at home in himself as he is playing. The intervals of silence and sound comfort his mind.

Together, we sing the familiar tunes of Bob Dylan, the Beatles, and James Taylor. He strums and together our voices fill our living room. I'll miss a beat, or he'll play the wrong chord, but it doesn't matter. The sweetness of comfort isn't about perfection, but about giving ourselves away to the music for a while.

Cultivating Comfort

Feel the comfort of music by listening to something that is special to you. It may be a song that holds memories, or one that you like to dance to. It could be your favorite music to sing along with, either by yourself or with others. What music brings you comfort?

Journaling

Reflect upon and write about the ways music comforts you, both when you're by yourself and with others.

Meditation & Prayer ♥

As I play a piece of music that touches me deeply, I close my eyes and sink into listening as a sacred experience, allowing the music to reach deep within and take me on a journey.

History

I pull one of the photo albums off the bookshelf. Our albums from over the years are lined up like the books of our lives. Some in cloth covers, others in vinyl ones, some on my phone, and others on my computer. Mostly they are filled with photographs of vacations and trips, family gatherings, and holiday events.

As I look through the pages of one of the albums, the comfort of memory comes over me. I feel myself tracing my history, connecting the dots of my life. In our albums are many photographs of people with food, either at restaurants or holiday parties. At every family event, my mother has us hold up our plates before we eat so she can take our picture. I usually roll my eyes at her request, and yet these are some of the most memorable photographs to look at afterward.

Sometimes, I will say to my husband, "Let's look at a travel album." We lean back on the sofa and begin the journey. Ah, New York City, 1989. Look, there we are, back onto the streets of New York, up to the Empire State

Building, and into the glow of Times Square. Suspended into our memories, alive and vibrant, time feels more elastic. The memories are comforting. Sharing a history with someone is comforting.

Cultivating Comfort

Comfort can be found in the memories you hold and in the stories of your life. Open a photo album and let yourself drift into the pictures. Feel the comfort that is created through good memories.

Journaling

Reflect upon and write about the comfort you find in photographs that hold your story. You can also choose a specific photo and write about the memories it evokes.

Meditation & Prayer 💜

I remember someone special that I share a history with, and let love fill me with a deep sense of comfort. I invite a prayer of gratitude to arise in my heart for this relationship.

Hold Me

*S*o if you don't want me to solve your problem or give you advice, what do you want me to do?

Comfort me.

How?

Hold me.

Let me talk.

Be soft.

Be gentle.

Be present.

We lean into the intimacy of wanting comfort, and create it for each other. We ask. We try. We are discovering how to comfort one another.

Thanks.

That's what I needed right now.

Cultivating Comfort

It is only by opening yourself to the need for comfort that you will ever experience it. Can you allow comfort to soften what is hard, warm what is cold, and sweeten what is bitter? Do you need to ask for more comfort in your life? What stops you? What supports you? Reach out to one person you trust and ask for comfort.

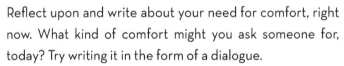

Journaling

Reflect upon and write about your need for comfort, right now. What kind of comfort might you ask someone for, today? Try writing it in the form of a dialogue.

Meditation & Prayer

Sit in a comfortable position and take several deep breaths to relax. Place your hands on your lap, palms facing upward. With your hands and heart open, ask for and allow yourself to receive comfort.

Home

The comforts of home are felt in our bodies. They are held in the warm sheets of our beds and are shared at the tables where we eat.

The comforts of home live in the towels that dry our skin, the cups that touch our lips, and the chairs that hold our bodies.

The comforts of home are contained in the books that line the bookshelves and the paintings that hang on the walls.

The comforts of home are held in the framed photographs on the mantel, the silver candlesticks on the dining room table, and the open fireplace offering warmth. The comforts of home are found in the intimacy of laughter and talking during the day, and in the silence and stillness of the night.

The comforts of home are in the forgiveness we ask of one another and the love we give and receive every day.

Cultivating Comfort

Look at your home through the eyes of comfort. Is there something you need to do to feel more comfort in your home—clear out a closet, place a vase of flowers on a table, get a new set of towels, or say that you are sorry to someone you love?

Journaling

Reflect upon and write about your home as a source of comfort for yourself and others.

Meditation & Prayer

I feel deep gratitude for the comforts of my home—for the bed that gives me rest every night, for the cozy chair I relax and read in, and for the feeling of warmth and protection that my home gives me. Let me become more aware of all the ways that my home nurtures me.

27

A Journal

My journal is a secret companion, a book of blank pages in which anything and everything can be said. At times, the page is exploding with thoughts and ideas, while at other moments the page is quiet, tenderly feeling the sadness lining my heart. My journal invites me to speak and connects me to the comfort of listening to myself in a deeply personal way.

Since I was a teenager, I have written in journals. Over the years, my notebooks have collected bits and pieces of my life story. As I look through a filled journal, I'll find pages stained with tears, coffee, or red wine. I'll find pages with lists of groceries to buy, people to call, and errands to run. I'll find letters to God, letters to my mother, and pages with doodles or the latest version of my goals.

In the handwritten pages of my journals, I am hearing the comfort of my own voice.

Cultivating Comfort

Your voice is waiting for you. Can you give yourself the comfort of listening to it? Open a journal and begin speaking. Keep it simple, write for three to five minutes a few times a week, about everything and anything, from the experience of getting your hair cut to your craving for more affection.

Journaling

Reflect upon and write about how writing in your journal allows you to hear your own voice more clearly.

Meditation & Prayer

In the presence of the Divine, I connect with my desire to know myself more deeply. I pray to listen to what is in my heart.

Laughter

*L*aughter lifts the spirit and brings comfort. There are times when laughter comes easily. My husband and I will tell each other about the things that happened in our days, and find humor in the stories. Laughter warms us and brings us close.

Then there are times when laughter doesn't come easily. We lose our smiles and the worries in our lives overtake us. When that happens, we will watch a funny television show like *I Love Lucy*, or a Charlie Chaplin movie, and surrender ourselves to the comedy. Laughter returns and we comfort ourselves with its relief and enjoyment.

Cultivating Comfort

Laughter is a wonderful source of comfort. Tell jokes. Watch funny movies. Do silly things. Remember to laugh every day. It's as important as breathing. How do you bring the comfort of laughter into your life?

Journaling

Reflect upon and write about the ways laughter brings you comfort. You may also want to write about the last time you found humor in a situation and laughed at yourself.

Meditation & Prayer

May I hear the joy of laughter all around me today—from a child, from a friend, and from myself. And let me hear the great laughter of God, inviting me to relax and let go more. I pray to open up to and embrace more laughter in my life.

Light

hen I was a girl, I kept a flashlight near my bed, and read by its light when my sisters were asleep. I was attached to that flashlight and found comfort in knowing that it was always within my reach. Now, whenever I go to a hotel, I always bring a flashlight and keep it on the bedside table.

A flashlight. A candle. A crackling fire. Light envelops us, holds us, embraces us. Light brings us comfort. In the morning, as a shaft of light streams into the bedroom, and I recognize it's a new day, I receive the gift of life that the light brings.

Cultivating Comfort

Invite the beauty and comfort of light into your daily life. Take time to notice the golden light of the sun, and the white light of the moon. Watch the way a shadow changes the depth and color of a mountain. See the light reflecting in a pool of water or shimmering through the leaves of a tree. Can you find ways to bring more light into your home, either natural light, or candlelight, or soft light? Let the comfort of light fill you.

Journaling

Reflect upon and write about the ways you connect with comfort through the gift of light.

Meditation & Prayer

I remember that in the darkness the light still burns within. May divine light bring hope to my places of darkness.

A List

There is a comfort in creating lists and carrying them around—in a notebook, a pocket, or a wallet. A list is a friendly helper. My favorite kind of list is an "Enjoy Life" list:

- ✧ Smile at someone
- ✧ Kiss your beloved
- ✧ Enjoy eating an apple
- ✧ Take a walk
- ✧ Look up at the sky
- ✧ Look at a tree
- ✧ Daydream and let your mind relax
- ✧ Laugh at yourself

Cultivating Comfort

What would be on your "Enjoy Life" list?

Journaling

Reflect upon what kind of list would bring you the most comfort, then start writing that list.

Meditation & Prayer

May I enjoy the many gifts in my life, and remember the comfort and joy they offer me every day. I pause, and take a deep breath, appreciating the pure gift of breathing.

Listening

There is a source of comfort naturally available to us through the way we respond to each other in our daily lives. Comfort can be found and given with a warm smile, through a gentle touch, and by genuine listening. Comfort comes from the words that are exchanged in the hallway at work, in a conversation over lunch, or on the telephone.

"Oh, I didn't sleep well last night," a colleague says to me.

"I have trouble sleeping sometimes; it's rough," I say.

We chat for a few minutes about being up at night, flipping through magazines, and worrying about not sleeping enough. We even share ideas that have helped us.

"Hang in there," I say.

Yes, there are big problems, global concerns, but there are also our everyday problems, the soil that we live in. Taking a moment to care and feel for one another creates a culture of comfort.

"I need comfort, but I don't even know how to get it," my

friend tells me. She is in pain. She and her husband are not communicating well these days. They are under the strain of financial pressures.

I listen. Listening is a form of comfort. Sometimes there is only the listening, nothing else. Through my listening, I hope to make the room feel really large, so that my friend doesn't feel she needs to run and hide.

Comfort is as small as it is big. It's a word of reassurance and a cup of tea, or a box of tissues and a long phone call.

Ultimately, we comfort ourselves by comforting others.

Cultivating Comfort

Comfort comes through listening, both to others and your-self. Listen to what wants to speak in you. It may be your body asking you for attention, your thoughts wanting to be expressed, or your heart needing some tenderness.

Journaling

Reflect upon and write about how listening to yourself—your body, your thoughts, and your heart—brings you comfort.

Meditation & Prayer

I listen as a way of praying: listen to what my heart is longing for, listen to what my body is asking me for, listen to the whispers of the Divine calling me closer.

Comfort and Joy

Love

The comfort of love fills me, the way sunlight fills the sky. It spills over and flows into everything—into the ground where we walk, and the air that we breathe.

The comfort of love reaches me in the warm sun and the sweet embrace of intimacy. It dwells deep in the compassion of my heart. The comfort of love expands far beyond what my naked eye can see, or what my bare hands can hold.

The comfort of love is simple and bold, forever present in our lives.

Cultivating Comfort

Connect to the rich sources of love that are in your life. Can you receive the comfort of love that is all around you?

Journaling

Reflect upon and write about the sources of love in your life.

Meditation & Prayer ♥

May I trust love today at every turn, during moments of happiness as well as moments of sadness. I let my heart be held in God's loving embrace, where every part of me is accepted, received, and loved.

Moments

There is a woman named Pam who goes to the public pool where I swim several times a week. In the locker room, a wonderful sense of female community and intimacy is created as the women shower, slather on lotion, and comb their hair in the open space. The women are always chatting. There, I've often spoken to Pam about her life and mine. She has been in chronic pain for several years from a back injury.

One Sunday, on the way home from having lunch with a friend, I decided at the last minute to go to the pool for a quick swim. I always keep a bathing suit and towel in the trunk of my car. In the locker room, after my swim, I heard a voice greet me. It was Pam. As we were showering, she announced that it was her birthday, at which I joyously exclaimed, "Happy birthday!" But Pam was not joyous. She told me that for the first time, her age was really hitting her. She was forty-six, without a partner, never having had children.

As I got in my car and began to drive away, a feeling gripped me. This is real life. Give comfort when you are called. Respond. I remembered the silver and white scarf I had just bought at a local store. I turned my car around and pulled up in front of the pool. I raced up the stairs and back into the locker room. I handed Pam the scarf. We hugged. As I drove home, my heart felt the power of comfort. Comfort pours joy, love, and care back into the world.

Cultivating Comfort

Throughout the day, there are many moments calling you to give comfort. They often happen in the midst of our busy life—in the hallway at work, walking down the street, or when a friend calls as you're rushing out the door. Pay attention to the moments in your life that are full of comfort possibilities.

Journaling

Reflect upon and write about the ways you're called to give comfort to others.

Meditation & Prayer 💜

May I be a living source of comfort to others, and grow in my capacity to love my neighbor as myself.

Mornings

I drink a cup of hot, black tea every morning, always with milk and a touch of sugar. Why do I always have my tea the same way each morning? There is a comfort in the repetition. No matter how poorly I slept, the cup of tea anchors me to my body and to the currents of time. I sip, and as the warm liquid soaks into my mouth, quenching my morning thirst, I am awakened to a new day.

Holding the cup of tea, the world feels recognizable and familiar. We seek this comfort almost immediately as we awake from the strangeness of the night, not really knowing where we have been.

I drink tea in a house in Mexico, a café in Prague, a hotel room in Canada, and every morning wherever I may be. Always, the experience of drinking my morning tea runs deep, connecting me to myself and comforting me. And in those moments when I drink tea with my husband or a friend, and we catch a glimmer in each other's eyes after the first sip, there is an unspoken comfort that we share together.

Cultivating Comfort

Your everyday routines can be a continual source of comfort. How many times has that first sip of coffee or tea in the morning brought you pleasure and comfort? How many times has snuggling into your bed at night given you comfort? What other moments in your day bring you comfort?

Journaling

Reflect upon and write about your everyday routines that are a continual source of comfort in your life.

Meditation & Prayer 💚

I allow my simple morning routines to deepen and become sacred moments. I choose not to rush through my morning tea or coffee but pause and linger, letting the moment reach deeply into my body and soul.

Mothering

After my sister died of cancer and I began to suffer with insomnia, I spent more time talking with my mother, either on the telephone or while visiting her in Palm Springs. "You're going to be just fine. It will pass," my mother told me time and time again. Just hearing her reassurance gave me comfort.

Mothering is a source of comfort, at any age, and in many forms. I feel it with my husband, when he brushes my thick brown hair, or makes blueberry pancakes for breakfast. I find it with a friend, as she gives me advice over a long lunch of Caesar salads. A teacher's praise is mothering. A doctor's patience is mothering. A hairstylist washing my hair is mothering. A neighbor giving me lemons from her garden is mothering.

There is a mothering quality in each of us, man or woman, and tapping into that, feeling that, can give great comfort. We find it in a tone of voice, in a touch, in words, in silence. And we find it in ourselves, when we are alone.

Cultivating Comfort

Mothering is something you need at any age. Can you expand your notion of how and where you can experience mothering? Self-nurture can be a generous form of mothering, so take time for a relaxing bath, or spend a few extra minutes brushing your hair, or treat yourself to a leisurely lunch. Can you find comforting ways to give yourself the love and patience you need right now?

Journaling

Reflect upon and write about the ways that mothering yourself and others gives you comfort and joy.

Meditation & Prayer

May I listen to the way life is calling me to be a mother today, to care for those around me, to be patient and strong. May I be a mother to myself, and listen to the places in me that are asking for my care and comfort. I pray to respond to myself with tenderness and understanding.

A Name

The other day, a bank teller recognized my name because it was also her daughter's name. "Oh, she spells it the same way too," she told me. In that brief moment, we connected in a warm and comforting way, sharing the intimacy of a name together. It made me realize that a name is both personal and part of the collective at the same time.

A name is given to us. I always like hearing my mother tell the story of how I was named after the French saint from the fourteenth century, and not the promiscuous French writer of the twentieth century. My mother, who is passionate about the lives of saints, named all her children after saints from various centuries and different countries.

We can never own our names. We share them with people throughout time and space, connecting us to the comforting web of human life.

Cultivating Comfort

Do you know the story of your name? Find it out and share it with someone. Knowing the story of your name can be a personal source of comfort, and connect you more deeply to yourself. Through the story of your name, you may find a connection to your ancestors, or to historical and creative people. Hear the gift of your name. Listen to the way different people say it. What comfort can you discover in the story and sound of your name?

Journaling

Reflect upon and write about the comfort you find in your name.

Meditation & Prayer ♥

I pray to hear the sacredness in my name, and to trust that I am part of the holy web of life.

Napping

I reach over and pull the cream-colored blanket over my husband's shoulder. It is a Saturday afternoon and we are taking a nap, an interlude from the day. Waking up twice in one day is a wonderful way to erase the marks of time.

I like napping in other rooms in our house besides the bedroom. Sometimes, I nap on the couch, or in the soft lounge chair in the office, or on a pile of blankets on the living room floor in front of a crackling fire.

I find comfort in listening to my body and not pushing myself all the time. When I nap, I always remove my shoes and my watch. Even if I don't fall asleep, as soon as I shut my eyes, there is an instant relief in letting go and feeling my body stop in repose.

There is a comfort in napping that I have felt for a long time. It lives deep in my memory. I remember dozing in the car on the way home from school, or on the sofa while watching an afternoon television program. Regardless of the sounds around me, I would sink into myself and drift away. Now on the weekend, or on vacation, I take the time to rest, to give my body and mind a comfort break.

Cultivating Comfort

Resting is an ancient art, one that has been lost in the busy demands of daily life. Taking time to relax the body and stop is an instant form of comfort. Is there a way you can find rest during the day? Close your eyes at your desk for a few minutes, sit in the car and take a few deep breaths before driving to your destination, and when possible, carve out time on the weekend to take your shoes off and nap.

Journaling

Reflect upon and write about the ways resting can provide you with deep and nourishing comfort.

Meditation & Prayer

I invite myself to rest in the care and comfort of Spirit. I pray for the willingness to let go more deeply, and allow divine love to envelop me and bring me ease.

Open Door

I will now say to my husband, my sister, my friend, or to myself, "I need comfort." And although saying these words makes me feel vulnerable, I have decided to embrace them. For the door to comfort has opened many times through vulnerability.

Slowly, I kept opening this door in me, inviting more comfort into my life. I craved tenderness, and at times it was so difficult to feel. I put my ear to my heart and listened. I was trusting the growing urge of instinct that was leading me to this open door.

One ember of vulnerability guided me to this door. I was opening it, and I was opening myself to comfort, the light glowing in the darkness.

Cultivating Comfort

Can you open the door to comfort in your life? There are many doors of comfort waiting to be opened by the reach of your heart and the stretch of your hand. Comfort is always available to you.

Journaling

Reflect upon and write about the ways you can open yourself more fully to the comfort that is available to you.

Meditation & Prayer

In moments of vulnerability, may I open the door of my heart and dwell more deeply in all that comfort is offering me.

Pillow

I place my pillow in the perfect spot under my head and sink into its softness. My pillow is a nightly source of comfort. It is a trusted friend that hears my bedtime whispers as I say goodnight to my husband and quietly say a prayer of gratitude for the day.

Ever since I went through a period of insomnia, I now take my pillow with me whenever I travel. I will often omit an extra pair of pants or shoes just to fit it in my suitcase. In a strange room and an unfamiliar bed, my pillow comforts me with its familiarity, holding the scent of my skin and the secret language of my dreams deep within its core.

Every day, as I make my bed, I take a moment to fluff up my pillow and smooth out the pillowcase. I pay attention to take care of what is taking care of me, and in that exchange there is a quiet feeling of comfort.

Cultivating Comfort

Allow yourself to feel the comfort being offered to you through everyday objects, like your pillow, your coffee mug, or your hairbrush. What simple and ordinary things give you comfort in your daily life? Can you take notice of them and recognize the comfort they are providing to you?

Journaling

Reflect upon and write about the objects in your life that are always offering you comfort.

Meditation & Prayer

I say a prayer of thanksgiving for the many objects that surround me and give me comfort every day in so many ways. May I take time today to stop and recognize them.

Prayer

*P*rayer is public, and prayer is private. It is words, and it is silence. I surrender to prayer's mystery. I close my eyes and let my small self slip away. I am ocean, sky, mountains. I dwell in the mystery of what I can't entirely grasp, and connect with something much larger than myself.

Sometimes, I doubt the act of praying, but that doesn't stop me, because there in the deep chambers of my heart, I feel the great force of love.

I do not try to squeeze myself into the frame of faith that has been built for me over the centuries. I let faith become larger than what I can know or understand. I let the expansion, not the limits, create my experience.

My mother once told me that prayer is a commitment to love. I didn't quite understand what she meant, but it kept me thinking. Now, I feel the pull of love drawing me like a magnet into the circle of humanity, held together by the comfort of prayer.

Cultivating Comfort

The very act of lighting a candle is a prayer. As you light the candle, you rekindle the divine flame that dwells within you and all around you. Take time to light a candle and connect with the comfort it is offering you.

Journaling

Reflect upon and write about the ways that praying provides you with comfort. Is there a special prayer that comes to mind?

Meditation & Prayer

I pray with my desire to connect more intimately with my life as a sacred journey.

Rain

I am crying, feeling the deep sadness that loss brings. I call my friend and we go for a walk. It is a cool and overcast day, so we bundle ourselves in jackets, scarves, and hats. Afterward, sitting in my kitchen, we share a pot of tea. I feel the warmth on my fingers as I cradle the mug. It begins to rain.

The rain is comforting—the tapping on the window.

When it rains, I feel a soothing passage of time. I don't feel anxious about time the way I often do when I am consumed with my goals and measuring my life against them. When it rains, time feels right, and that's such a relief. It is time for it to rain, and it rains.

My friend and I stay in all afternoon. Being inside when it rains produces an uncompromising sense of comfort. We are protected by the warmth and shelter of my home. I cry. We talk. We listen. It is reassuring to cry when it rains. The rain and my teardrops create a rhythm, a syncopation. Finally, the rain clears. My tears soak into the earth. And nature has washed the sidewalks, the streets, and my sticky, muddy heart.

Cultivating Comfort

Nature is a reminder of the cycles in life. There is sunshine and rain, laughter and tears, morning and night. Can you be as patient and present as the rain? Can you connect to the comfort of nature?

Journaling

Reflect upon and write about finding comfort in expressing your feelings, and in particular your tears.

Meditation & Prayer

May I receive comfort and joy during this season of my life. I let the rain nourish the soil of my soul.

Reading

I spend an afternoon reading a novel, absorbed in the life of a fourteen-year-old girl who lives in South Carolina and is learning about beekeeping. This is thousands of miles away from the urban, forty-something life I live. The world of the imagination is an immeasurable source of comfort. I like to lose myself in a novel, enter into a private world where a month passes in a page, a decade in a chapter, and a century by the end of the book.

There is an intimacy in reading, in the way the book feels in my hands; the characters fill my imagination, and the ideas interact with my mind. A book becomes a companion for a while, waiting with me at the airport, sitting with me in a café, or lulling me to sleep at night. A book is a source of comfort in everyday life.

So while the neighbors are washing their cars and weeding their gardens, I am spending a Saturday afternoon with a teenage girl in the South, immersed in the world of my imagination and enjoying its comfort.

Cultivating Comfort

The imagination is a gateway to new possibilities, inviting you to look up at the scattering clouds changing shape in the sky. Your imagination is freely available to you. How are you allowing it to comfort you?

Journaling

Reflect upon and write about the ways your imagination can bring you comfort.

Meditation & Prayer

I pray with the dreams and desires I hold for my life. I trust in my imagination to allow me to see myself in a more expansive way.

Shoes

There's a pleasure in wearing a comfortable pair of shoes. Sometimes, no matter what I am wearing, or what I'm doing, if my feet feel at home in my shoes, then I am at home in myself.

I slip into my pair of coffee brown suede loafers. The shoes meld to my feet after months of wear. Finally, just right. Enjoying the ahh I feel every time I slip into them. My shoes know me, my personality, my habits, and my obsessions. They stand in line with me at the grocery store, walk the four blocks from the bus stop to the office building, and spend the day with me at my desk dealing with deadlines. On the soles of my shoes, I can trace the maps of my days.

I hear the sound of my shoes walking on cement, hardwood, or linoleum. I feel my feet stepping onto the ground, pushing into the dusty and soft earth. My shoes protect my feet and toes, stained with loving and living. Even though I have many pairs of shoes, I end up wearing the same ones over and over again. Comfort needs to be held really close, inseparable from the body.

Cultivating Comfort

Your shoes are one of the most intimate items you wear every day. How you feel in your shoes affects how your entire body feels. Through your shoes, you connect to the Earth and the ground that you walk on daily. Do you have shoes that give you personal comfort every time you put them on?

Journaling

Reflect upon and write about your shoes as a source of comfort. You may also want to write about one of your favorite pairs of shoes and the places you go together.

Meditation & Prayer

May I feel my connection to the ground I walk upon, and with every step receive the comfort it offers.

Smells

When I was a child, before my mother went on a trip, she would give me a white handkerchief scented in her perfume, Chanel No. 5. I would place it under my pillow, and when I missed her, I'd cover my face with the piece of cloth and inhale her scent. I can still close my eyes and smell that handkerchief.

The smells of comfort are held in the body. "You smell so human," my husband says to me. He brushes his cheek against mine, delighting in the sweet oil of my skin, mingled with the warm air and dry grass after hours of walking in the open hills.

Daily smells are a constant comfort. As I walk up the steps of my house, I smell the salty sea air lingering from the ocean just a mile away. In the living room, I can smell last night's fire. In the garden, I smell wet grass, and the bedroom still smells of the sandalwood incense I had been burning. For me, these are the smells that tell me I am home.

We punctuate our days with the comforting smells of food, from freshly baked blueberry muffins in the morning to garlic and basil cooking in a tomato sauce in the evening. A whiff, a waft, a sniff, and the scents carry and soothe.

The smells of comfort live deeply inside of us, held in our bodies and in our memories.

Cultivating Comfort

Through the senses you take in the world around you. The sense of smell is very powerful and can bring you reassurance and pleasure. The scent of oranges, chocolate, or the ink of a new book can connect you to a deep-dwelling place of comfort. What smells connect you to comfort, what smells give you comfort?

Journaling

Reflect upon and write about the smells that comfort you. You may want to write about one smell in particular and the memory it evokes.

Meditation & Prayer

My senses invite me into a moment of prayer, and I take delight in my sense of smell. What scent am I enjoying at this moment? I allow this noticing to become a prayerful moment.

Comfort and Joy

Solitude

*S*ometimes I am the only one who can give myself the comfort I need. There is a private comfort that I find in my own company. I feel it when I take a long, meandering walk, silent and alone, drifting in and out of my reveries. I sense it when I sit quietly in the comfortable chair in my bedroom, or when I take a long, slow bath.

Layer by layer, I peel away what's covering me—the worries, the fears, the comparisons—and settle into my own solitude. Finally, I find my skin, my breath, my voice. In this interior dwelling, I can hear my voice saying, I am here.

I ask myself, *What do you need right now?* It may be tenderness, acceptance, courage, action, silence. I take time to enjoy the sweet company of my solitude, to listen to my voice, and learn to recognize its unique sound.

Cultivating Comfort

Taking time to be alone is important for your health. A deep, satisfying comfort emerges when you learn to be with your own company and listen to your own needs. Ask yourself, What do I need right now? There are times when you need to focus on what you can do for yourself, and not on what you expect from someone else.

Journaling

Reflect upon and write about how solitude is, or can be, a great source of comfort in your life.

Meditation & Prayer ♥

I invite myself to embrace quiet moments, daily. I relax into the comfort they offer me. When I notice them, I pause and say, "Thank you."

Sounds

I hear the sounds of comfort:

✧ The echo of my voice singing under a stone archway

✧ The smacking of my lips as I kiss my sweetheart

✧ The sounds of water, gushing over rocks, crashing on the shore, whispering on the edge of a fountain

✧ The chirping of sparrows hovering around the bird feeder in the backyard

✧ The cathedral bells ringing loudly through the streets as I am walking

✧ The warm tone of my father's voice

✧ My hand scratching pencil marks on newsprint as I am drawing

✧ My own breath, moving in my chest and through my nose

✧ And the silent sounds, like the full moon on a clear night, or my husband's hazel eyes looking at me like the stars

Cultivating Comfort

Listen to the orchestra of sounds all around you every day. Hear them. Enjoy them. Let them catch your attention, bring you delight, and spark a moment of comfort. What particular sounds bring you comfort?

Journaling

Reflect upon and write about the comfort you find in different sounds.

Meditation & Prayer ♥

As I listen to the sounds around me, they become prayers—the tapping of the rain, the chirping of a robin, my husband's voice.

Stillness

I walk in a redwood grove, where giant sequoia trees have lived for hundreds of years. Because the trees are so large, the sight of tree trunks dominates my vision. There they stand, still and silent. Their stillness slows me down.

I sit and absorb the trees, feel the roots in my feet, the base deep in my belly. In the simple act of sitting, ease settles into my body, and there, comfort can find room.

Stillness comforts. I sit in a museum and look at a painting. I sit and absorb the colors, shapes, lines, feeling, and tone of the painting. I look, not intent on knowing whether it's a Matisse or Picasso, but taking it in whole, unnamed, poetic and dreamy.

Still. Present. Allowing time to stop. Comfort is always there ready to be tapped. Comfort lives all around us: in a chair waiting to be sat in, a tree waiting to be looked at, in the eyes of a painting calling us inside.

Cultivating Comfort

Just like a tree needs room to grow in the ground, comfort needs room to grow in your life. Imagine yourself planted firmly into the earth like a large tree. Can you connect with the stillness that is inside of you? Sometimes by stopping and being still, you can recognize that comfort is right in front of you.

Journaling

Reflect upon and write about the ways stillness can offer you comfort.

Meditation & Prayer ♥

I pray with the words, "Be still and know that I am God."

Talismans

I have a velvet pillow filled with buckwheat and scented with lavender that my husband gave me for a Valentine's Day present one year. It's designed as a roll to fit underneath my neck when I am reading in bed. Now, when I have trouble sleeping, I lay the pillow on top of my chest. Its weight and softness feel comforting. This simple pillow roll has now become an object of comfort for me.

There are things that comfort us by their presence: in our rooms, our cars, and our pockets. They remind us of special people, important moments, or powerful feelings. They are the silver candlesticks that belonged to our grandparents, a smooth stone picked up at the beach, the medal of a saint on a keychain, and the tattered photographs in our wallets. They are totems of comfort that we can touch and hold in our sight.

Cultivating Comfort

Imagine how many drops of comfort a day you are receiving from the presence of simple but sacred objects: a wedding ring, a bracelet, a photograph of a loved one, an icon. Take a look around you. Recognize the objects that are giving you comfort—privately, quietly, daily.

Journaling

Reflect upon and write about the totems of comfort in your daily life.

Meditation & Prayer

I hold a sacred object in my hands, with a deep sense of appreciation for the memories and meaning it embodies. I offer a prayer of gratitude for all the comfort it gives me.

Time Out

When my husband and I feel too much pressure from the demands of work, money, or keeping it together, we take time out.

We clear our schedules, make no plans, and let ourselves drift through a day. We'll start by having our tea and toast in bed, slowly and leisurely, reading books or the newspaper, and chatting about anything and nothing. Later, we might meander through the park on our bicycles, with no particular destination, stopping to look at the ducks in the pond or the wild ferns. By late afternoon, we'll take a nap, and then end the day eating slices of pepperoni pizza while watching a favorite old movie like *Breakfast at Tiffany's*.

It's comforting to take time out, in knowing this is what we need to do, and in doing it.

Cultivating Comfort

Not putting any expectations on yourself, even for an hour or an afternoon, is a simple way to bring yourself comfort. Can you find a way to clear your schedule and comfort yourself with time out?

Journaling

Reflect upon and write about the ways releasing expectations can soothe you with comfort. Write about one particular situation that is calling to you?

Meditation & Prayer

I pray to give myself permission to listen to my deepest desires, and respond to my need to simply be at times and not always do.

Toast

*I*was at a painting workshop in Big Sur, California. There we were, twenty grown-ups, spread out on the floor, each with a pocket-sized notebook and a box of eight crayons. The workshop leader was having us draw in our notebooks, quickly, with swift marks, which didn't give us time to say, "I can't draw that." We drew our most embarrassing moments, our favorite pair of shoes, our most comforting food, and more, until our books were filled with drawings about our lives.

We shared our notebooks, many of the drawings simple lines or abstract shapes. Everyone was laughing. When we got to the page of the most comforting food, I was amazed to see how many people drew pictures of toast. Piles of cinnamon toast dripping with butter. Toast with peanut butter and a glass of milk. Toast with strawberry jam.

The memory of eating toast is itself a comfort. At eight years old, I loved days in which I could come home right after school, change out of my uniform, and sit in front of the television, eating two pieces of white toast covered in butter and sprinkled with cinnamon sugar. Life was perfect for that one hour.

Even today, when my husband and I can't sleep, we find ourselves in the kitchen making pieces of toast, and eating them with glasses of cold milk. White, wheat, multigrain, challah, cinnamon raisin, rye. Butter. Jam. Marmalade. Peanut butter. Nutella. Eating toast feels comforting. It's soul food. It's something we have been doing since childhood.

So there we were, at the painting workshop at Esalen, staying up late and painting. Walking back to our rooms, we stop in the dining room, where a basket of bread is always out, sitting next to a toaster. With paint staining our fingers, we sit around a table eating toast and drinking milk, laughing and feeling comfort.

Cultivating Comfort

Let yourself appreciate the comfort of food in your life. The ambiance and the people you eat with can also create the comfort factor. Maybe you'd like to make a dish of your favorite comfort food, and share it with someone special in the comfort of your home. What foods truly comfort you?

Journaling

Reflect upon and write about the ways food nourishes your body and soul, and gives you comfort.

Meditation & Prayer 🤍

I feel gratitude for the comfort that my favorite foods give me. I allow the memory of sharing these foods with others to fill me with comfort.

Comfort and Joy

Touch

Sometimes comfort needs to be felt, needs to be physical. I think of Mother Teresa of Calcutta, her ministry to the poor, sick, and dying. It was a ministry of touch. Every time I see my elderly neighbor —who now lives alone after the recent death of her husband of sixty years—we exchange a gesture of caring. It's spontaneous. We squeeze hands, hug, or pat each other gently on the back.

We feel comfort through touch. I still hold my mother's hand. I've held her hand forever, crossing the street, walking in the park, sitting in the hospital after my father's heart attack. Her hands are warm and strong. Over the years, they have cleaned a lot of floors, folded piles of laundry, and stirred many pots. Her knuckles are thick like the roots of a tree.

To hold hands is a tender and intimate act. It is the child in us crawling into a refuge; it is the desire to connect; the desire for union in a very simple way. Sometimes, more than words, I desire the unspoken.

Cultivating Comfort

Touch gives comfort. A simple hug. A kiss on the cheek. A stroke on the arm. A handshake. A pat on the back. You connect through touch, and it is an instant source of comfort. How are you inviting touch into your life?

Journaling

Reflect upon and write about the ways touch is a source of healing and comfort in your life.

Meditation & Prayer

I am touched by Divine presence, and am filled with a sense of comfort and connection. Embracing my sense of connection with the sacred, I close my eyes and let a prayer arise in my heart.

Walking

*T*here is a trail near my house that I have walked on hundreds of times over the past ten years. I have walked there in rain, wind, sunshine, and fog. It's about three miles long and curves along a cliff overlooking the ocean. Wildflowers and bushes of fennel grow abundantly at different times in the year. Each time I start walking along this path, and the ocean air hits my face, I feel a comforting connection to myself.

Over the years, I have walked on this trail alone, with my husband, with family, and with friends. This path knows me. It has felt my silence, heard my voice, held my tears, and absorbed my laughter. It has heard me questioning my life time and time again.

Regardless of the weather, this trail is always ready to receive me and my desire for a walk. Some days, the ocean is calm, the sky is blue, and the smell of fennel fills the air. I walk more slowly, taking time to soak in the landscape. Other days, the wind is fierce, the sky is gray, and fog drips in the air. I walk quickly, without stopping, bundled in a jacket, scarf, and hat.

It is comforting to return to this trail again and again, to step on a soil that holds many moments of my life. Landscape is as interior as it is exterior, and in that dual relationship there is a deep, primal comfort.

Cultivating Comfort

A particular place or landscape can give you comfort. Take time to visit a landscape that is special to you. It could be a park, a garden, the ocean, the city streets. Notice the smells, the sounds, the colors, and what you feel about the place. How does it comfort you?

Journaling

Reflect upon and write about a particular place or landscape that brings you comfort.

Meditation & Prayer

Let me recognize the sacredness of the landscape that surrounds me, and enter the holy through the places I walk in my life. I am filled with awe and delight at the wonder of the earth that sustains me every day.

Whispers

My husband and I will often say to each other, "Let's chitchat." It's a code for taking time to care about the little things in our day. We take time to share the simple moments.

What did you have for lunch? Tuna salad and a bowl of soup.

Did you talk to your mother on the phone? She took my father to the doctor today.

How do you like your new shoes? They're great, really comfortable.

In soft voices that melt into the walls, we listen to each other. Someone caring about what you ate for lunch is pure comfort.

Cultivating Comfort

The simple act of listening to yourself and to another person creates a deep sense of intimacy and connection that comforts. Take time to listen, not while you're feeding the dog, or putting the groceries away, but when you can really be present in a relaxed way to what another person is saying.

Journaling

Reflect upon and write about the ways that moments of intimacy and connection in your daily life bring you comfort.

Meditation & Prayer ♥

I pray to recognize and listen to the whispers of spirit that lead me to greater intimacy with myself, others, and the Divine.

Bringing Comfort

Into the World

Living Comfort

*I*t was while I was visiting a monastery in rural Kentucky that I first realized how great a gift comfort had become in my life. I spent a week at the Abbey of Gethsemani: following the daily schedule of the monks, praying and chanting with them, eating my meals in silence, and walking through the golden leaves of the fall foliage in the woods and hills surrounding the monastery.

The monks follow the same simple rituals and routines, day after day, year after year. Daily they chant, pray, eat, sleep, cook, clean, and work in the fields, in the barn, or the factory making fudge or fruitcake. One afternoon, as my husband and I were finishing a walk through the gardens around the monastery, I turned to him and said, "I always love taking a walk with you."

In that moment, I realized that, just like the monks, I also engaged in the same routines and rituals every day. I've rediscovered these things as sources of comfort. Over and over, I have found comfort in a walk, in a bath, in a cup of tea, in a talk with a friend, in gardening, praying, and singing.

For me, it's not about constantly seeking new experiences for comfort, but in allowing the ordinary things in my daily life to fully resonate with the depth of comfort they had to offer. I have come to recognize that these daily experiences deepen over time, offering me the gift of comfort again and again.

Offering Comfort

*I*t has been a cold, wet winter for northern California. When I get home at the end of the day, I am acutely aware of the comforts of home—a warm shower, a companion to share dinner with, a cozy bed with layers of blankets. Each touch of warmth and softness is noticed and appreciated.

One morning, on my way to work, I stop at the local bakery. I notice a man sitting on the bench in front of the store, wrapped in a wool blanket and warming himself in the sun. As I am leaving, with my cup of coffee in hand, I turn to the man and ask him if he'd like a scone. "Sure, I'd love one," he replies. I bring him a scone and fresh coffee, too. We smile at each other, and in that moment I realize that my sensitivity to comfort in my own life has deepened my capacity to offer comfort to someone else.

We all need comfort. As children we reached for comfort easily and naturally, holding our parent's hand, hugging a teddy bear, or wearing our favorite pajamas night after night. Now, as adults, we still desire to feel comfort in our lives, but it is not always easy to give and receive it.

So how do we give comfort within the daily demands of our lives? In simple and practical ways. We share what we have to give. We offer a kind word, a smile, a hug, a caring heart, and an open ear.

We can share comfort in very immediate ways—as we stop and listen to another person, read a book with a child, take a moment to call an elderly parent, laugh with a friend, give a sandwich to someone sitting on a corner, or donate a coat to help keep someone warm.

Bringing comfort into the world is about paying attention to how and where the need for comfort is calling us: to a colleague who needs a word of support, to a person on the bus who needs a seat, to a spouse who's looking for encouragement, or to the neighborhood senior center looking for volunteers.

Simple actions. Wide ripples. Deep resonance. It only takes our mindful attention to connect to the comfort inherent in eating a warm bowl of soup, or holding hands with someone special, or walking in the park. Yet, it is not only the warm bowl of soup that gives us comfort, but also our willingness to notice and appreciate the healing and restorative gift offered to us in this very simple experience.

The more we bring comfort into our daily lives, the more we can share it with our families, friends, workplaces, communities, and the world around us. We can become messengers of comfort, and encourage others to replenish and nurture themselves in the everyday rituals of their lives. By recognizing what provides us with comfort and care, we can help others to tune in to the same transformative gifts of comfort in their lives.

One Sunday morning, as I sat in a chair in my living room, sipping my cup of tea and writing freely in my notebook, I could sense that these everyday rituals were giving me comfort.

Later, the phone rang, and it was my friend. She was brokenhearted over a relationship that had ended recently. She needed to talk. I listened patiently and compassionately, sharing her disappointment and sadness with her. She cried, and I held her tears in my silence.

She thanked me for listening. "How can you give your-self some comfort right now?" I asked. I reminded her of the comfort available in an afternoon nap, a warm bath, moments of silence, a long walk, time spent in nature, or helping someone. We talked about the need to restore ourselves with these gentle and nurturing activities.

The Gifts of Comfort

Because I have found comfort in the simple act of drinking a cup of tea, I can offer a friend a cup of tea and know that I am nurturing her.

Because I have discovered comfort by holding my aging mother's hand, I can share comfort with my elderly neighbor, who reaches for my hand during a walk together.

Because I have felt comfort in the act of compassionate listening, I can offer that comfort to my sister, who is crying during one of our phone conversations.

Because I have deeply experienced my own need for physical comfort, I can respond to a request for towels needed at one of the local shelters.

In all our daily relationships as a spouse, parent, relative, friend, colleague, and community member, there are many moments asking us to respond with tenderness, patience, encouragement, and reassurance. The more we cultivate comfort in our own lives, the more readily and freely we can bring these gifts to others.

Seen through this lens, we more clearly understand the connection between taking care of ourselves and taking care of others. They share the same root system. One allows for the other, and in my experience comfort is incomplete if it is kept only for oneself. The ability to respond to others with care and compassion is only enhanced by the extent to which we as individuals notice, nurture, and cherish the simple, everyday gifts that offer us their unending bounty of comfort and joy.

Applying Comfort

In Your Daily Life

Applying Comfort in Your Daily Life

Gestures of Comfort

∽ Practice small gestures of comfort: write a note to a friend for a recent accomplishment, call your grandmother on a Sunday afternoon, make a pot of soup and invite a friend for lunch, offer to pick up something from the grocery store for an elderly neighbor, light a candle for someone who needs your prayers.

∽ Hospitality is a gift of comfort you can offer others, whether they enter your home, your office space, or your studio or backyard. Create a space for people to sit, have a bowl of goodies available with chocolate or hard candies, and most important, have a welcoming attitude.

∽ Share a bouquet of flowers with different people who walk into your life. This can be spontaneous and unplanned. Give a few stems to a friend who comes over to dinner, or to the people who help you around the house, or to the next-door neighbor.

❧ Send a card, a note, or an e-mail to comfort someone. Remember a special occasion, acknowledge an accomplishment, offer support during a difficult time or transition.

❧ Is there something that has given you comfort that you could now give to someone else who is needing comfort? It may be a book, a picture, a figurine, a rosary, or a soft sweater. Offer this gift as a sign of support and caring.

Take a Comfort Break

- Encourage someone to take a comfort break with you. Go to a matinée movie, see an art show, take your shoes off and walk on the sand.

- Invite someone to share a walk with you in nature. Notice the flowers, trees, clouds, hills, or water that surrounds you. Recognize it. Appreciate it. Share it. Nature is a living source of comfort.

- Take a walk or sit in a place of comfort with someone: a rose garden, a cathedral, or a museum. Dwell in both the comfort of the place and in sharing it with someone you care about.

- Take a person you care about on a comfort walk—go to the beach, the park, or one of your favorite neighborhoods. Don't get caught up in talking about any problems, but rather appreciate the scenery together.

Comfort Through Creative Activities

ৎ Keep a comfort journal for a week. Every day write for five minutes. Put the word comfort at the top of the page and begin writing. Reflect on ways you are bringing comfort into your daily life. Reflect on how you are offering comfort to others.

ৎ Make someone a scrapbook or album as a gift for a special occasion. Make it as simple or elaborate as you'd like. You can use different things to fill the pages, like photographs, stickers, rubber stamps, magazine images, and words from quotes or poems. The person you give this gift to can enjoy its comfort for many years.

ৎ Singing with other people is a joyful source of comfort. It's easy to find lyrics to songs on the Internet. Print them out and start singing with friends, family, and children. Feel the enjoyment of sharing music with other people.

Comfort in Relationships

ᜃ Find a way to bring comfort to your partner: offer a foot massage, cook a favorite dinner, buy a single rose, be creative and personal.

ᜃ The next time you are at a family gathering, let the comfort of being with your family be stronger than judgment and criticism. Walk over to a relative, sit down, and enjoy a conversation, even if it's only about the weather or the food.

ᜃ Create a moment in the morning that brings comfort to those around you. Put out a bowl of fresh fruit on the breakfast table, give your spouse a good morning hug, say hello to the person serving coffee, or offer someone your seat on the bus.

ᜃ Imagine a thread connecting every human being. Connecting yourself to the web of life can provide comfort. We are not in each other's way, but we are the way for each other. We are the sources of comfort for one another.

Comfort in Community

❧ Spend a Saturday afternoon working in a community garden in your area, or participating in a beach cleanup. Connect with others to create something of beauty in the environment.

❧ Volunteer to read to children at your local library or elementary school. Enjoy the comfort of sharing a book with children, laughing over silly stories, asking questions, and looking at colorful illustrations.

❧ Gather a group of people together to make gift baskets. They could be baskets filled with toiletries to give to a local shelter, or baskets of flowers to bring to a nursing home, or baskets of fresh fruit to share at work.

Comfort at Home

⁙ A comfortable home benefits everyone who lives there and everyone who visits. Find easy ways to create more comfort in your home. Get new throw pillows for the sofa, put fresh flowers in a vase on the dining table, make Sunday morning breakfast, or clear out the linen closet and neatly fold the towels.

⁙ Create a sacred space in your house: a chair in your bedroom, a bench in your garden, or a corner of the sofa in the living room. There you can light a candle, read a prayer or a daily meditation, drink your tea, write in a journal, or sit in silence. Remember other people during this time, offering prayers, blessings, or gratitude for them.

⁙ Give someone the gift of a beautiful bowl to put on a table—a dining table, kitchen table, bedroom dresser, or desk. It could be a large or small bowl. Tell the person it's an offering bowl, to remind her of the importance of giving and receiving, and of remaining in a posture of openness.

∽ If you know a friend is needing a little extra comfort, invite her over for a home spa experience. Pamper yourselves with delicious things like a papaya face-mask, a soothing menthol foot soak, or a cocoa butter hand treatment. End with a period of deep relaxation by resting in silence for ten minutes.

Comfort Through Sharing Food

&s Pack yourself and your family members some snacks to enjoy during the day. A simple thing like a box of raisins or a bag of walnuts can bring comfort to a long afternoon. It's not only the snack, but the gift of feeling cared for that produces comfort.

&s From time to time, bring a treat to share with people in your daily life. Putting out a jar of almonds or a plate of cookies on the table in the lunchroom creates an atmosphere of comfort and community. It will catch on, and other people will share in the idea, and soon more people will be smiling in the hallways.

&s Remember that the environment and the people you eat with can enhance the comfort factor. Make a favorite recipe, set the table with candlesticks, and enjoy sharing the meal with good company. The layers of comfort will make the meal a feast for everyone.

Comfort Through the Senses

୬ There are many ways to bring the gift of touch into other people's lives. Comfort can be given in a simple hug, a kiss on the cheek, or a gentle touch on the back. It can be felt in a pair of cashmere socks, a velvety fern plant, or a soft stuffed animal. Discover all the comforting ways to bring touch into people's lives.

୬ The next time you are shopping with someone for clothes, put the focus on what textures and materials feel comforting. When the person asks, "How does this look?" you can add the question, "Does it feel comfortable?"

୬ Give a present that evokes the comfort of scent. Find a sachet filled with French lavender, an assortment of organic mint teas, a teddy bear, a dozen fragrant roses, or a jasmine plant. Let your nose be your guide.

୬ Share the comfort of sounds with other people. Next time you are taking a walk and hear a woodpecker tapping on a tree trunk or church bells ringing, stop, stand still, and enjoy listening together. Did you hear that?

Comfort Through Evoking Memories

    Ask an older person, a parent, grandparent, neighbor, or friend, about something he liked to do as a child, such as a favorite hobby or pastime. Watch the person's face light up with the memory, and share in the joy of hearing his story.

    Find some photographs of yourself as a child, perhaps during a vacation, a holiday party, or any event that brought you happiness. Share the photographs with your children, or your partner, or a friend. Enjoy the comforting feeling of remembering and sharing a good memory from your childhood.

Comfort Through Greater Awareness

✎ Gaining awareness of comfort only increases the support and softness that comfort can offer you and others. So the next time you are with someone and experiencing a comfort moment, simply stop and say, "This is comforting." Take a moment to recognize it together. Yes, this is comforting.

✎ For a day, notice all the little ways you can offer comfort. You might help someone cross the street, bring home an apple pie for dessert, make a donation to a charitable organization through their website, wait patiently while everyone gets into the car in the morning.

✎ What are some ways to mother yourself with comfort? Make a list: buy some new pajamas, get new linen for your bed, go out to dinner with a girlfriend, commit to a writing or art class. What are things you could do for someone else? Make a list: take someone out to lunch, encourage someone's creative expression, be patient with someone's struggle, give reassurance that a problem will find a solution.

ও Discover the comfort of gratitude. Throughout the day, express gratitude: say thank-you in a genuine way to the people around you, to your partner, to a colleague who listens to a problem you are having at work, or to your child who brings you a picture she made for you at school.

Comfort Through Acceptance

∾ For one day, don't say anything critical or judgmental about a special person in your life, either out loud or to yourself. Instead, replace the critical thoughts with the words, *I love and accept you.*

∾ Receiving the presence of another person's tears is a great gift of comfort to give someone. Allow the person to cry, without judgment or interruption. Let the tears become part of nature. Sometimes there's nothing to figure out, it just needs to rain tears.

∾ Give the gift of an unhurried presence to another person. Can you be with someone and sip your tea, stroll in the park, and not try to make anything happen or to change anything?

Comfort Through Listening

～ Be quiet for five minutes and listen to your calling for comfort. Be quiet for five minutes and listen to someone else's need for comfort.

～ Listen to another person without any pressure to give advice or solve a problem. Allow yourself to lean back, let go, and give the person plenty of room. Listening is enough. Sometimes all another person wants is the comfort of being listened to, without interpretation or interruption.

～ Today when you ask someone, "How are you?" take the time to really listen. Slow down for five minutes and be present. Listening to another person is a true gift of comfort in our busy world.

Comfort Journaling Prompts

1. Reflect upon and write about one area in your life in which you could be more accepting. What would that look and feel like?

2. Reflect upon and write about one of your favorite daily rituals and how it brings you comfort.

3. Reflect upon and write about the ways you open yourself to receiving comfort.

4. Reflect upon and write about the places where you find comfort.

5. Reflect upon and write about a transition you are experiencing, and the ways that comfort is a circle holding you during this time.

6. Reflect upon and write about the ways you are held in comfort by what you wear, both during the day and at night.

7. Reflect upon and write about how doing something creative brings you comfort, such as cooking, gardening, singing, writing, or drawing.

8. Reflect upon and write about the ways you experience comfort in nature or in applying an awareness of the cycle of life to a personal situation.

9. Reflect upon and write about the ways you can give yourself comfort today.

10. Reflect upon and write about the ways music comforts you, both when you're by yourself and with others.

11. Reflect upon and write about the comfort you find in photographs that hold your story. You can also choose a specific photo and write about the memories it evokes.

12. Reflect upon and write about your need for comfort, right now. What kind of comfort might you ask someone for, today? Try writing it in the form of a dialogue.

13. Reflect upon and write about your home as a source of comfort for yourself and others.

14. Reflect upon and write about how writing in your journal allows you to hear your own voice more clearly.

15. Reflect upon and write about the ways laughter brings you comfort. You may also want to write about the last time you found humor in a situation and laughed at yourself.

16. Reflect upon and write about the ways you connect with comfort through the gift of light.

17. Reflect upon what kind of list would bring you the most comfort, then start writing that list.

18. Reflect upon and write about how listening to your-self—your body, your thoughts, and your heart—brings you comfort.

19. Reflect upon and write about the sources of love in your life.

20. Reflect upon and write about the ways you're called to give comfort to others.

21. Reflect upon and write about your everyday routines that are a continual source of comfort in your life.

22. Reflect upon and write about the ways that moth-ering yourself and others gives you comfort and joy.

23. Reflect upon and write about the comfort you find in your name.

24. Reflect upon and write about the ways resting can provide you with deep and nourishing comfort. You may also want to write about how you can find more moments of rest in your life.

25. Reflect upon and write about the ways you can open yourself more fully to the comfort that is available to you.

26. Reflect upon and write about the objects in your life that are always offering you comfort.

27. Reflect upon and write about the ways that praying provides you with comfort. Is there a special prayer that comes to mind?

28. Reflect upon and write about finding comfort in expressing your feelings, and in particular your tears.

29. Reflect upon and write about the ways your imagination can bring you comfort.

30. Reflect upon and write about your shoes as a source of comfort. You may also want to write about one of your favorite pairs of shoes and the places you go together.

31. Reflect upon and write about the smells that comfort you. Write about one smell in particular and the memory it evokes.

32. Reflect upon and write about how solitude is, or can be, a great source of comfort in your life.

33. Reflect upon and write about the comfort you find in different sounds.

34. Reflect upon and write about the ways stillness can offer you comfort.

35. Reflect upon and write about the totems of comfort in your daily life.

36. Reflect upon and write about the ways releasing expectations can soothe you with comfort. Write about one particular situation that is calling to you.

37. Reflect upon and write about the ways food nourishes your body and soul, and gives you comfort.

38. Reflect upon and write about the ways touch is a source of healing and comfort in your life.

39. Reflect upon and write about the ways touch is a source of healing and comfort in your life.

40. Reflect upon and write about a particular place or landscape that brings you comfort.

41. Reflect upon and write about the ways that moments of intimacy and connection in your daily life bring you comfort.

Comfort and Joy

About the Author

COLETTE LAFIA is a San Francisco-based spiritual director, workshop and retreat facilitator, and writer. She is also a part-time school librarian. Colette is the author of *Seeking Surrender: How a Trappist Monk Taught Me to Trust and Embrace Life*, and *Comfort and Joy: Simple Ways to Care for Ourselves and Others*. She has a sincere passion for helping people connect more deeply with the presence of the sacred in their daily lives and blogs about it at www.colettelafia.com.